paper
scissors
glue

catherine woram

photography by
polly wreford

paper
scissors
glue

**45 fun and creative
papercraft projects for kids**

RYLAND
PETERS
& SMALL
LONDON NEW YORK

Senior designer Toni Kay
Commissioning editor Annabel Morgan
Location research Jess Walton
Production Toby Marshall
Art director Leslie Harrington
Publishing director Alison Starling

Stylist Catherine Woram

First published in 2010
by Ryland Peters & Small
20–21 Jockey's Fields
London WC1R 4BW
and
519 Broadway, 5th Floor
New York, NY 10012
www.rylandpeters.com

10 9 8 7 6 5 4

Text, design and photographs
© Ryland Peters & Small 2010

ISBN: 978-1-84597-975-1

Library of Congress Cataloging-in-Publication Data

Woram, Catherine.
  Paper scissors glue : 45 fun and creative papercraft
projects for kids /
Catherine Woram ; photography by Polly Wreford.
      p. cm.
  Includes index.
  ISBN 978-1-84597-975-1
  1. Paper work. I. Title.
  TT870.W657 2010
  745.54--dc22
                                        2010009607

Printed and bound in China.

contents

introduction

If your kids loved *Crafting with Kids* and *Christmas Crafting with Kids,* then they are sure to love this new addition to the series. *Paper Scissors Glue* is the perfect choice for the thrifty crafter, as many of the projects can be made with a few scraps of paper and card. Of course, the most important equipment is a big pot of glue and some scissors, as well as paint, brushes and decorating items.

The book covers many traditional paper-crafting techniques, ranging from cutting and folding to sticking, printing and papier-mâché. There are also some very simple origami techniques. From a 3-D dinosaur cut from coloured card and then slotted together to egg-carton insects, pretty beaded necklaces and pop-up cards, the projects are guaranteed to appeal to both boys and girls aged from three to ten years and beyond.

Each project is accompanied by four clear and simple step-by-step photographs and there are often suggestions for other items that can be made using the same technique, as well as handy tips. You will find that many of the projects are surprisingly cheap and easy to make and that the basic items required may already be in your craft box or cupboard. No specialist equipment is required, and any templates needed are included at the back of the book, along with a handy list of suppliers that specialize in crafting materials.

During the photography, it was a delight to see how much all the child models enjoyed the actual crafting processes involved. The sheer look of deep concentration on their faces in some of the photographs bear testament to this! I am sure you will enjoy helping your child or children with the projects in this book and that they will enjoy making the items, playing with them and proudly presenting them as gifts to friends and family.

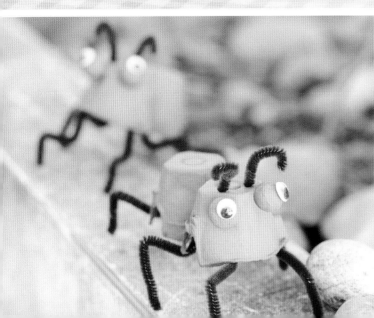

cutting

YOU WILL NEED:

plain paper for template • scissors • pieces of decorative paper – gift wrap is ideal • pencil • pinking shears • PVA/white glue • ribbon to fit length of bunting required

create template Photocopy the template on page 118 and cut it out. Place the template on the back of a piece of decorative paper and draw around it in pencil. It is quicker to draw all the triangles at once, then cut them all out in one go.

cut out bunting Cut out the triangles using pinking shears. Alternatively, use plain scissors or the decorative-edged scissors that feature designs such as scrolls and scallops and which can usually be found in craft shops.

make paper fold Fold the wide base of each triangle over to the wrong (unpatterned) side, following the fold line shown on the template. Run your finger along the fold to flatten the paper.

glue to ribbon Run a line of glue along the inside of the paper fold. Lay the ribbon on this then fold the paper over flat. Press down and hold in place until the two sides of paper stick to the ribbon. Leave a gap of about 4cm/1½in of ribbon between each triangle. Continue to stick triangles to the ribbon until you have created the required length of bunting.

paper bunting

This fun paper bunting is made using decorative papers featuring flowers, spots and checks for a fun and colourful look. You can make the bunting as long as you like – just carry on sticking the bunting triangles to the ribbon until you have finished.

ladybird mobile

This cheerful mobile with its bold dotty ladybirds would look great hanging in a window or from a lampshade in a bedroom.

YOU WILL NEED:

paper for template • scissors • pencil • 1 piece A4/letter-sized red card stock • 1 piece A4/letter-sized black card stock • PVA/white glue • nylon thread • red paint • paintbrush • 2 wood battens measuring 1cm x 1cm x 20cm/½in x ½in x 8in • white paint

create template Photocopy the ladybird template on page 118 twice and cut the templates out. Draw around the body template on red card stock and around the face and spot templates on the black card stock. Draw a second set for the other side of the ladybird.

cut out shapes Cut out the ladybird bodies, head and spots. If preferred, you could use black self-adhesive dots for the ladybird spots.

decorate ladybird Glue the face and six spots to one side of the ladybird, as shown. Turn over and repeat on the other side. Repeat these steps to make three more ladybirds. Paint the wooden battens red and ask an adult to drill a hole through the middle of each piece and at each end.

finishing Use a fine paintbrush and white paint to paint on the eyes. Allow to dry completely. Stick the battens together in the shape of a cross, lining up the central holes. Push through a loop of nylon thread to hang the mobile from. Make a hole at the top of each ladybird and use nylon thread to attach a ladybird to each of the four ends of the battens.

YOU WILL NEED:

photocopy of photograph
of a head in profile • 1 piece
of coloured paper • pencil •
decorative paper • picture
frame • buttons to decorate •
PVA/white glue • scissors

cut out silhouette Use scissors to carefully cut out the photocopy of the head in profile. For very intricate areas, you may want to ask an adult to help you by cutting out the silhouette using a sharp craft knife.

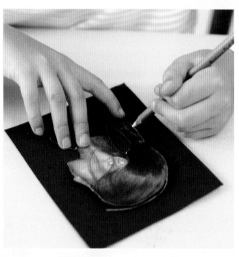

draw around silhouette Place the cut-out silhouette template on the back of the coloured paper and use a pencil to carefully draw around the shape. Again, cut out using scissors or ask an adult to help you with a craft knife.

glue to paper Apply glue to the back of the shape. Stick it firmly to the decorative paper and press flat. Allow the glue to dry completely. If required, paint the frame to coordinate with the silhouette and decorative paper that you have chosen.

finishing Decorate the frame by sticking on a selection of pretty buttons with glue or a hot glue gun (a hot glue gun must only be used by an adult). Leave the frame to dry completely. Insert the silhouette and close the back of the photograph frame.

silhouettes

The traditional craft of cutting out paper silhouettes is both fun and easy, and they make great gifts for friends and family, especially grandparents. Simply photocopy a photograph of your own profile, then cut it out in coloured paper and glue it to a decorative background paper. You can use the same technique to decorate boxes, books and cards.

decorated box

Cut out part of your silhouette to decorate a lidded box and finish it off with a border of coordinating gingham ribbon glued down one side. A band of ric rac trim running around the lid adds a decorative flourish to finish this pretty jewel box.

mother's day card

A perfectly pretty card for a mother, this silhouette was mounted on polka-dotted patterned paper and a dainty velvet bow was used to adorn the hair.

little tips

When choosing a suitable photograph for the silhouette, make sure that your profile is clear and sharp. You may find it easier to start from scratch and ask someone to take a photograph of your profile close up against a white background, so that your features are easily seen.

secret journal

Make a secret journal for a close friend or for yourself by sticking a silhouette to the front of the book and finishing with a border of fancy felt braid. Cover the book in pretty coloured paper before fixing the silhouette and add ribbon ties glued to the inside of the cover.

paper weaving

Paper weaving is a simple and effective paper crafting technique. The end result can be used to decorate many items to create attractive and practical gifts (see pages 20–21). We used odd buttons, self-adhesive dots and pretty ric rac trim to adorn this woven paper mat.

YOU WILL NEED:

4 pieces A4/letter-sized paper in different colours • pencil • ruler • scissors • PVA/white glue • 2 60cm/24in lengths of ric rac braid in different colours • self-adhesive dots • decorative paper • buttons

cut out paper Using a pencil and ruler, draw strips on the back of the different-coloured pieces of paper, making sure that each strip is approximately 2.5cm/1in wide. Using scissors, cut out the strips.

start weaving Lay two different coloured strips of paper at right angles to each other and glue together. Then glue another strip of paper below the top horizontal strip, running parallel to the vertical strip. Now stick a second, horizontal strip to the underside of the vertical strip. Use alternate colour strips and repeat the technique. Weaving the strips under and over each other creates a sturdy mat of woven paper.

continue weaving Continue to weave the strips over and under each other. As you reach the end of the original strips, stick the edge of the strip you are working to either the top or underneath of the original strip and press it down flat. You may need to trim the ends of the strip to make the edges tidy.

finishing When you have stuck down all the ends of the paper strips, decorate the woven paper mat. We used pretty buttons, which were stuck to each corner on top of a square of polka dot paper. Ric rac trim can be woven through the mat, while self-adhesive dots make a fun finishing touch.

pen pot

A cardboard tube (the sort used to hold potato snacks) can be transformed into a handy pen pot. Cut the pot to the desired height, then decorate it with a piece of woven paper made using the weaving technique. Finish with a pretty band of felt.

handy notebook

Cover a plain notebook with a woven panel and glue on a band of felt braid to make a lovely handmade gift. A piece of card woven with a single strip of paper makes a handy matching bookmark too. Simply cut slits in the card bookmark and weave a paper strip through from front to back. Glue the top and bottom of the strip at the back of the bookmark.

pencil box

Paint a wooden box in a colour that matches one of the paper strips. Measure the lid then weave a panel to fit, to create a simple yet decorative pencil box.

little tips

When covering an item such as a box or front of a notebook, it is better to measure the width and length and divide this measurement equally to make sure the paper strips will fit. If they are between 2–4cm/1–1½in wide, then they will look fine.

YOU WILL NEED:

plain paper for template •
scissors • pencil • 1 piece
A4/letter-sized green card
stock (for the large-size
crocodile) • 2 googly eyes •
PVA/white glue • white paint •
fine paintbrush

create template Photocopy the
template on page 123 and cut it out
using scissors. Fold the green card
stock in half lengthways and place the
template on top, lining up the crocodile's
spine with the fold of the card, as shown.

snip spiky spine Use scissors to cut out the
crocodile. Create the spiky spine effect by marking on
the lines as indicated on the template. Snip along the
lines through the fold of the card stock. Using a small
pair of scissors will keep the cuts neat and tidy.

fold spine Open the crocodile out flat. The cuts will have created six
triangular shapes. Fold these back on themselves, pressing them flat with
your finger. Carefully fold the crocodile in half again so that the knobbly
spines stand up all the way along the crocodile's back.

finishing Glue a googly eye to
each side of the crocodile's face.
Using a fine paintbrush, paint on the
crocodile's teeth using white paint.
You may find it easier to draw the
shape of the teeth onto the card in
pencil before you paint them.

cheeky crocodile

These fun crocodiles feature knobbly spines, toothy grins and googly eyes – make them in different shades of green and an assortment of sizes as decorative additions to your bedroom.

dotty flowers

These cheerful dotty flowers are made from
three heart-shaped pieces of card decorated
with self-adhesive dots. Create them in zingy shades
and paint paper cups to act as decorative pots.

YOU WILL NEED:

plain paper for template •
scissors • pencil • 3 or 4 pieces
A4/letter-sized coloured card
stock • self-adhesive dots •
PVA/white glue • strong/tacky
glue • fabric flowers • pipe
cleaners for stems

create template Photocopy the
heart template on page 119 and cut it
out using scissors. Place the template
on a piece of the card stock and draw
around it with a pencil. Repeat until you
have sufficient heart shapes (you will
need three per flower). Cut out the
hearts carefully with scissors.

stick on dots Peel off the self-adhesive dots and stick
them onto each heart. We used contrasting-coloured dots
for extra impact. Press each dot down firmly using your
finger to make sure they are securely fixed in place.

glue flowers together Lay three hearts together with the pointed
edges slightly overlapping to form a flower shape. Stick the edges together
using a dab of PVA/white glue and press firmly in place. Repeat for the other
flowers. Leave to dry completely.

finishing When the flower is dry, stick
a fabric flower in the middle with strong/
tacky glue and leave to dry. Use the
same glue to attach a pipe cleaner to
the back of each flower to act as a
stem. You could paint paper cups in
bold designs to hold your flowers.

YOU WILL NEED:

paper for template • scissors • pencil • pale and bright pink card stock • sharp thick needle • piece of firm foam (same size as star shape) • PVA/white glue or glue stick • glitter • strong/tacky glue • ribbon

cut out template Photocopy the star template on page 123 and cut it out using scissors. Place it on the back of the card stock and draw round the template with a pencil. Draw around all your stars before you cut them out to save time. You will need six stars of each shade (12 in total) to make the garland.

cut out stars Cut the stars out using scissors. For a more decorative effect, you could use pinking shears or scalloped-edge scissors.

pierce design Place one of the stars onto the piece of firm foam – this makes piercing the holes easier and prevents the card from creasing. Push the needle carefully through the card from the front to back and pull out. Make the next hole approximately 3mm/⅛in away from the first, and continue to pierce holes all the way around the edges of the star until finished.

finishing Draw circles in the middle of each star using PVA/white glue. Sprinkle with glitter and leave to dry. To string the garland put a blob of strong/tacky glue on the back of a star point and stick to the ribbon. Continue sticking until the garland is finished.

star garland

Simple card stars cut from bright and paler pink card
look delightful when pierced with a large needle to create
a delicate lacy finish. Decorate the stars with glitter and
string them up on ribbon to create this pretty garland.

stained-glass butterflies

This classic paper craft will enchant younger children. Shapes such as butterflies and hearts (as well as the more traditional stained-glass windows) look great cut from black paper and filled with pieces of brightly coloured tissue paper glued to the back of each shape.

YOU WILL NEED:

plain paper for template •
scissors • pencil • 1 piece
A4/letter-sized black paper
for each shape • white pencil •
coloured tissue paper •
PVA/white glue • black pipe
cleaners

create template Photocopy the template on page 119 and cut it out using scissors. Place the template on a piece of black paper then draw round it using the white pencil (to make the butterfly shape easier to see).

cut out butterfly Use the scissors to cut out the butterfly shape from the black paper. If you are making more than one butterfly, it is easier to cut out all the shapes at once before cutting the holes and sticking on the tissue paper.

draw shapes Using the white pencil, draw softly rounded shapes onto the back of the black paper butterfly. Use scissors to carefully cut out these shapes, which form the holes for the tissue paper.

finishing Cut out pieces of tissue paper that are just slightly bigger than the openings and glue to the back of the butterfly shape. Use only a tiny amount of glue, as too much will cause the tissue to get wet and tear. Finish the butterfly with two black pipe-cleaner antennae attached with blobs of glue.

YOU WILL NEED:

paper for template • scissors • pencil • decorative paper in a variety of designs • wooden tray • PVA/white glue or glue stick • water-based acrylic varnish • paintbrush

create template Photocopy the diamond-shaped template on page 118 and cut it out using scissors. Place the template on the decorative papers and draw around it using pencil. Repeat until you have enough diamonds to cover the bottom of the tray.

cut out patchwork shapes Use scissors to carefully cut out the diamond shapes. We used origami paper which features decorative patterns, making it perfect for this project.

glue shapes to tray Before you begin sticking the diamond shapes to the tray you may find it useful to lay them out on the tray first to create a pleasing arrangement. Lift each piece of paper individually to apply glue and stick to the tray, so you remember where each shape should go. Use your fingers to press the glued diamonds flat so they are firmly stuck down.

finishing Trim the diamond shapes to fit at the edges of the tray. The easiest way to do this is to lay them on the tray and fold back the edge of paper to the required place, then trim with scissors and glue in place. When the glue is dry, apply one or two coats of water-based acrylic varnish to finish.

découpaged tray

This tray has been découpaged with pretty patterned paper diamond shapes that were glued to the tray then finished with varnish. It's the perfect gift for a grandmother or for Mother's Day.

découpaged picture frame

Bring the traditional découpage method up to date by decorating a plain frame with simple square and rectangular pieces of bold paper decorated with attractive designs. We finished the frame with ric rac trim and cute buttons.

YOU WILL NEED:

decorative paper in a variety of designs • scissors • picture frame with wide edges for découpage • PVA/white glue • ric rac trim to fit frame • buttons to decorate

cut out shapes Cut out a selection of squares and rectangles from the decorative paper and arrange the pieces in piles of the same design to make sticking them easier. You may like to arrange the paper on the frame before you start sticking to work out your design, or you can simply begin sticking and see where you end up!

start sticking Begin sticking the shapes on the frame. Apply glue to the back of each paper square or rectangle. Press the edges of the paper flat with your fingers to make sure they don't curl up. Continue sticking on the shapes until the frame is completely covered.

decorate Apply glue to the back of the buttons and stick them on the frame at regular intervals. You could ask an adult to do this using a hot glue gun, as the glue sticks get very hot.

finishing Cut four lengths of ric rac to fit around the frame aperture. Use PVA/while glue to stick the ric rac to the frame, neatly bordering the aperture. Leave to dry completely. Insert a picture in the frame to finish.

YOU WILL NEED:

plain postcards and matching envelopes in two colours • ruler • pencil • decorative hole punch • eraser • box to hold notelets • PVA/white glue • scissors • braid or ric rac trim

mark spaces for punching

Use a pencil and ruler to mark the centre point on each card, about 1cm/½in down from the top. Now make a mark either side of this point, evenly spaced between the centre and edges of the cards. These are the positions for punching the designs on the notelets. Repeat for each notelet.

punch shapes Push the notelet inside the decorative punch in the position marked with pencil and push down firmly on the punch. Repeat the punching for the other two marks. When the punching is completed, use the eraser to remove any visible pencil marks from the card. We also punched the pointed corner of the envelope backs to match.

decorate box Use one of the unpunched notelets to stick to the front of the box and stick the punched shapes from the second colour to the top. Press down firmly to make sure they have stuck down properly and leave glue to dry.

finishing Cut a length of braid to fit the circumference of the box lid and use glue to stick it to the lid. Allow the glue to dry completely then fill the box with the punched notelets and matching envelopes.

paper notecards

Paper punches come in a huge variety of shapes and sizes. We used a flower-shaped punch to decorate these cute notecards, then used the punched-out flower shapes to decorate the box to make a pretty gift.

landscape collage

Use scraps of paper, card and tissue paper to make this bright collage showing a country scene complete with trees, flowers and a tiny cottage. You could also use scraps of fabric, ribbons and buttons, if preferred.

YOU WILL NEED:

1 piece card stock 50 x 50cm/20 x 20in • 1 piece blue paper 50 x 25cm/20 x 10in • paper for template • pencil • scissors • PVA/white glue • brown and grey card stock • plain and patterned paper • green tissue paper • paint • paintbrush

cut out cottage Glue the smaller blue 'sky' piece of paper to the sheet of card and allow to dry. Photocopy the house and roof templates on page 123 and cut them out using scissors. Place the template on the plain card and draw around it using pencil. Use scissors to cut the two shapes out. Glue the house and roof in the middle of the card.

make trees Cut out two tree-trunk shapes from brown paper and glue on either side of the cottage. For the leaves, scrunch small pieces of green tissue paper into balls and glue them in place to form an oval 'tree' shape.

continue decorating Cut out leaf and petal shapes from plain and patterned paper and stick to the bottom of the collage. Glue them together in groups for more effect, and finish the flowers with the addition of a coloured button at each centre.

finishing Use paint and a fine paintbrush to add detail to the collage. Add roof tiles, windows and door to the cottage as well as birds in the sky and white fluffy clouds. When the collage is complete, you can back it on stiff card if required, to make it sturdy enough to hang on the wall.

YOU WILL NEED:
cardboard tubes • scissors •
ruler • paint • paintbrush •
ric rac trim and ribbon •
PVA/white glue • buttons

cut out bracelet Cut open the
cardboard tube in a straight line using
scissors. Then measure approximately
5cm/2in in from the bottom of the
cardboard roll and cut along this line
to make a single bracelet.

paint bracelet Paint the cardboard roll both inside and
out with your chosen colour of paint and leave to dry thoroughly.
If better coverage is required, apply a second coat of paint and
leave to dry. You could also paint designs on the roll, such as
flowers or spots, before decorating with buttons and braid.

decorate bracelet Cut the ribbon and ric rac braid to fit the
circumference of the bracelet. Run a line of glue down each length of ribbon
and braid and glue in place, pressing firmly in position to flatten any wrinkles
out. Leave to dry completely.

finishing Once the glue is completely
dry, stick a row of buttons around the
top and bottom edge of the bracelet.
You may wish to use a hot glue gun
but if so you will have to ask an adult
to help, as the glue gets very hot.

cardboard
tube bracelets

These pretty bracelets are
made from cardboard toilet
paper cylinders. They make
great bracelets when painted
in zingy colours and decorated
with ribbon and buttons. They're
also a great craft project for a
children's party – little girls will
love to take these home.

folding

origami whales

These fun whales are made using a very simple origami technique. Make them in different sizes to create a whole school of whales to play with, and paint your own blue sea using a piece of textured handmade paper!

trim paper Lay the paper flat on a table in a diamond shape, with one point towards you. Fold the two outer corners towards the centre so they meet, and press the edges in place. Fold the bottom point tip of the paper up to meet the bottom of the two other folds.

fold body Now fold the piece of paper in half along the central axis with the existing paper folds on the inside of the paper and press all the folded edges down firmly.

fold tail Measure approximately a third of the way along from the pointed end of the folded body. At this point, fold the tail upwards at right angles to the body of the whale to form a tail. Now fold the tail over to the other side.

finishing Open out the whale and push up the tail section inside the body. Use scissors to snip a 2cm/¾in cut in the very end of the tail so that it can be folded outwards to create fins. Use a pen to draw eyes on the whale or stick on self-adhesive googly eyes.

YOU WILL NEED:

paper for template • scissors • pencil • white paper (we used wallpaper lining paper) • decorative paper • PVA/white glue • marker pens for faces • gingham ribbon for bows, 5mm/¼in wide

create template Photocopy the doll template on page 123 and cut it out. Fold the paper into concertina pleats, making each panel the width of the template. Place the template on the folded paper and draw around it. Make sure that the doll's hands extend to reach the folded edges of the panel.

cut out Using scissors, cut out the paper doll carefully. Make sure you do not cut along the folds where the hands and the hems of the dresses touch, so the dolls 'hold hands' all in a row when cut out.

decorate Trace the dress, shoe and hand shapes from the template onto the back of some decorative paper and cut out one outfit per doll. Apply glue to the back of the cut-out shapes and stick to the dolls, smoothing flat with your hands. We used different patterned papers for the dress, shoes and hands on each doll.

finishing Use the marker pens to draw eyes, nose and a mouth on the face of each paper doll, and add rosy cheeks too, if you like. Tie small gingham bows from the ribbon and stick two on each doll's 'bunches' to finish.

paper doll chain

This very cute traditional paper doll chain was cut from folded layers of paper and decorated with dresses and shoes made in decorative paper then finished with hand-drawn faces and ribbon bows. Use the chain to decorate shelves or hang it up like bunting.

folded paper fan

Made from a length of pleated paper, this fan is decorated with flowers, ribbons and glitter. Held together with two long sticks, it would also make a great decorative wall decoration.

YOU WILL NEED:
1 piece of paper 20 x 140cm/
8in x 4½ft • marker pen •
PVA/white glue • gold glitter •
2 wooden battens measuring
2.5 x 40cm/1 x 16in •
6 pieces ribbon measuring
1 x 30cm/½ x 12in

fold paper Place the piece of paper flat on the table in front of you. Starting at the end closest to you, make concertina-style folds that are about 2.5cm/1in wide. Press each fold flat. You can leave the pleated paper under a heavy book overnight to make it as flat as possible.

draw flowers Open out the paper so that it is almost flat and use the marker pen to draw flowers all over the paper at evenly spaced intervals. Apply glue to the centre of about five or six of the flowers and cover with glitter. Pour off the excess glitter and set it aside to reuse on remaining flower shapes.

continue decorating Repeat until all the flower centres are covered in glitter. Allow glue to dry completely. You can add further decoration such as leaves and painted decorations to the fan if you like.

finishing Place the two wooden battens together, then glue the two ends of the pleated paper to the sides of the battens. Leave the glue to dry. Now glue three lengths of ribbon to the top of each stick for a finishing touch.

YOU WILL NEED:

plain paper for template · scissors · pencil · pieces of A4/letter-sized coloured card stock · eraser · squares of decorative paper 15 x 15cm/6 x 6in (we used origami papers) · black marker pen

create template Photocopy the bird template on page 118 and cut it out. Place the template on a piece of coloured card stock and draw around it using pencil.

cut out bird shape Use scissors to carefully cut out the bird shape. Use an eraser to remove any pencil marks from the back of the cut-out birds.

fold wings To make the wings, take one of the squares of decorative paper. Starting at the end closest to you, make concertina-style folds that are approximately 2cm wide. Press each fold flat.

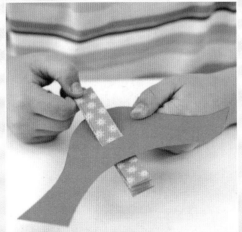

finishing To insert the wings, cut a slit on the bird's body exactly as indicated on the template. Slide the folded wing section through the slit, then open out the pleats slightly to form the bird's wings. Finally, draw on the bird's eyes using a marker pen.

paper birds

These delicate paper birds look great made in colourful card with brightly patterned wings. They would be equally delightful made from white paper for a wedding or christening, or from red and green paper to decorate the Christmas tree.

paper plane

One of the most traditional paper crafts, paper planes
have long been a favourite with boys, who will play with
them for hours. They're less popular with teachers when
they appear from nowhere during a class though!

YOU WILL NEED:
1 piece A4/letter-size coloured paper • marker pens

make first fold Lay a piece of paper horizontally in front of you. Use a ruler to mark the centre of the paper. Draw a faint guideline if necessary. Now fold one of the corners nearest you into the guide line. Firmly press the fold. Repeat with the other corner and firmly press the fold flat with your finger.

fold paper to inside With the folds uppermost, again fold the edges in once towards the central line and firmly press the folds flat.

continue folding Turn the paper over, then fold it in half on itself and press flat. This forms the basic shape of the aeroplane.

finishing Pinch the lower section of the 'plane' between your fingers and open up the 'wings', so they form a flat horizontal surface. Now decorate the wings of the aeroplane, if you like. Your plane is all ready for flying!

YOU WILL NEED:

1 square of patterned origami paper (approximately 20 x 20cm/8 x 8 in) • marker pen

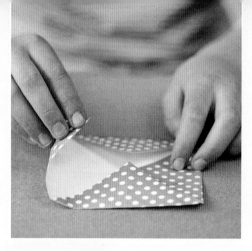

fold in corners Fold the square of paper in half one way then open it out and fold it in half again the other way. Now fold each corner of the paper into the middle of the paper and press all the edges flat by running your finger along the creases.

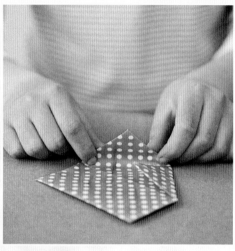

fold other side Turn over the paper to the other side. Again, carefully fold each corner into the centre of the paper and press the edges flat carefully using your finger.

fold in half Fold the paper in half along the straight edge and press flat. Open it out. Now fold it in half again the other way. Open out again. You will now have four flaps. Place your thumbs and index fingers inside the flaps and use them to open and close the fortune teller.

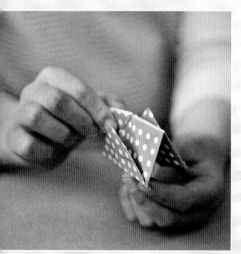

finishing Open out the fortune teller again. Write four numbers (or colours) on the top of each flap with a pen. Now turn it over so you can see the eight triangular flaps inside. Write a number on top of each flap and a fortune underneath it. You're all ready to play!

fortune tellers

These paper fortune tellers are great
fun to play with friends – each flap is
numbered and conceals a different
fortune. Make them using pretty
decorative papers such as origami
paper, which comes in dainty designs.

party bag cones

These card cones with handles are trimmed with dainty braid and make a perfect party bag when filled with yummy sweet treats. You could also make them from black and orange card stock to hold Halloween treats.

YOU WILL NEED:

1 large dinner plate to use as a template • pencil • scissors • 30cm/12in square piece card per cone • stapler • ric rac trim • PVA/white glue • sweets and chocolates to fill

draw out shape Use the plate to draw a semicircle on the piece of card and cut out with scissors. You will need one semicircle of card stock per cone. For each cone, you will also need to cut a handle measuring 2 x 20cm/1 x 8in from the card.

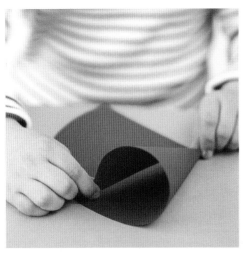

roll into cone Roll the card into a cone shape making sure you hold the pointed end firmly with one hand. Use the stapler to staple the cone together at the top. You may find it easier to do this if an adult holds the cone for you.

glue on trim Measure the top of the cone and cut a piece of ric rac trim to the same length. Apply glue to one side of the trim and stick around the top of the cone approximately 1cm/½in down from the top of the rim. Press down firmly with your fingers and allow the glue to dry.

finishing Apply a blob of glue to the top and bottom edges of the handle section. Stick to the inside edge of the cone and press firmly in place. Fill the cones with a selection of sweets and small chocolates to finish.

YOU WILL NEED:

2 pieces paper in two different
shades green • scissors • glue
stick • green pipe cleaner •
2 googly eyes • black pen

glue strips together Cut two
strips of paper (one of each colour)
measuring 2.5 x 30cm/1 x 12in. Lay
the two pieces of paper flat and at
right angles, with the ends overlapping.
Glue the ends together then press
down firmly and allow the glue to dry.

start folding When the glue is completely dry, fold
one length of the paper over the other so that it lies flat at
a right angle to the other. Continue folding until you have
formed the pleated body of the caterpillar. Trim the ends
of the paper if necessary, so they are perfectly square.

glue the ends Glue together the ends of the caterpillar. Press
them together firmly and allow the glue to dry completely. You may
find it easier to staple the ends of the caterpillar together, but
remember you will be able to see the the the staples.

finishing Stick the googly eyes
to one end of the caterpillar and use
a pen to draw on a nose and mouth.
Snip a few pieces of pipe cleaner.
Apply a dab of glue to the end of
each piece and tuck inside the layers
of paper, just above the eyes, to finish.

cheeky caterpillar

This jazzy little caterpillar is made from two lengths of paper folded together and finished with big googly eyes and caterpillar antennae.

pirate hat

Made from plain black paper, this fun pirate hat is created simply by folding a single piece of paper. Decorate with stamped skull and crossbones motifs.

YOU WILL NEED:

1 piece of A2/16½ x 23⅛in black paper • pencil • PVA/white glue • white or grey card scraps • skull and crossbones rubber stamp • black inkpad

start folding Lay the paper on a flat surface with the short end facing you. Fold the paper over on itself along the long side, like a book. Press flat. Now open the paper out and fold the other way – fold the top down to the bottom edge and press flat.

continue folding Fold the two top corners inward and down to the central line. Press flat using your fingers. You should now be able to see the hat shape.

fold brim Working on the top side of the hat, fold the bottom edge up to meet the bottom of the triangles. Now fold it up once again. Turn over the hat and repeat on the other side. This is the brim. You may want to use a dab of glue or tape on the inside of the brim at each end to hold it in place.

decorate and finish Cut out three circles of paper with a diameter of approximately 7cm/3in. Print the skull and crossbones designs using the rubber stamp and inkpad. Leave to dry completely. Glue the badges to the front of the pirate hat to finish.

YOU WILL NEED:

plain paper for template •
scissors • pencil • 8 A4/letter-
sized pieces decorative paper
per bell • glue stick • ribbon •
strong/tacky glue • beads •
strong thread

create template Photocopy the bell template on page 119 and cut it out using scissors. Place the template on the back of the decorative paper and draw around it using pencil.

cut out bell shapes Use scissors to carefully cut out the bell shape. In total, you will need eight bell shapes for one finished bell, and it's easier to cut out all the shapes in one go.

fold bell shapes Fold each bell in half lengthways, making sure the pretty pattern is on the inside. Glue one half of a bell to one half of the next bell and press flat with your fingers. Continue to glue the bell shapes together, pressing down firmly as you work.

finishing When you reach the last two bell shapes, cut a length of ribbon and stick it to the inside of the top of one side with strong glue. Thread three beads onto thread. Tie a knot in one end of the thread and glue the other end to the inside of the bottom of the bell. Stick the last two sides of the bell together and leave to dry.

paper bells

These decorative paper bells are made by sticking eight bell shapes together and look great in pretty pastel designs but equally good in shades of silver and gold as festive Christmas decorations.

chinese dragon

Make this bold and dramatic
Chinese dragon using a length of
pleated paper and a cardboard
head and tail and decorate it with
colourful tissue-paper streamers.

YOU WILL NEED:

1 piece of card stock 20cm x 75cm/8 x 30in • paint • fine paintbrush • pencil • paper • scissors • 2 pieces of A4/letter-sized red card • orange and white paint • PVA/white glue • strong/tacky glue • 2 wooden battens • coloured tissue paper • four or five lengths of ribbon

create body Place the large piece of card stock on the table, with the short edge in front of you. Make 5 even folds, turning the card over each time to create a concertina effect. Using a paintbrush and red paint, paint differently sized dots onto the card. Let the paint dry completely.

cut out face and tail Photocopy the dragon templates on page 122 and cut them out using scissors. Place the template on the red card and draw around it using pencil. Cut out the dragon's eye carefully (it may be easier for an adult to do this using a craft knife).

decorate face and tail Use a paintbrush and paint to decorate the dragon's face and tail as desired. When the paint is completely dry, glue the head to one end of the folded card stock, and the tail to the other end. Use strong/tacky glue to fix the wooden battens to the wrong side of the card, positioning one at each end of the main folded length of card.

finishing Cut strips of tissue paper and stick them beside the dragon's mouth on the wrong side of the card, to create a 'breathing fire' effect. Glue or tie the lengths of ribbon to the wooden battens to finish.

YOU WILL NEED:

plain card stock • scissors • pencil • paper • paints • paintbrush • rubber

create template Photocopy the Christmas tree template on page 119 and cut it out using scissors. Place the template onto a folded piece of card stock. Draw around the template in pencil, lining up the long edge of the Christmas tree template exactly with the fold of the paper.

cut out tree shape Using scissors, carefully cut around the tree shape, making sure you do not cut through the two sections at the bottom of the tree marked on the template. These two sections keep the pop-up tree attached to the card itself. If you find it difficult to cut out the tree, you may wish to ask an adult to cut it out for you using a craft knife.

fold out design Open out the card carefully and push the Christmas tree shape forwards so that it stands away from the folded card to create a 3-D effect. Now you can see how important the uncut side sections are, because they keep the tree shape attached to the card.

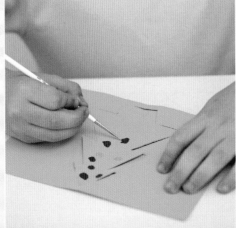

finishing Use a fine paintbrush to draw spots on the tree to depict decorations, Add small gift boxes scattered around the tree to finish the card. You can add glitter if desired for a more sparkly festive effect.

pop-up cards

These jolly 3-D cards are easy and fun to make and decorate. Try different designs for many occasions, including Christmas and Easter, and they also make great birthday cards and thank-you notes for family and friends.

magnetic bookmarks

These handy decorative bookmarks
are cut from the folded edges of cereal
packets. They are finished with pretty
patterned papers then trimmed with
decorative edging scissors.

YOU WILL NEED:

an empty cereal box •
• scissors • decorative paper
(we used gift wrap) •
glue stick • pinking shears •
self-adhesive magnets

cut up box Cut out a rectangular shape from the cereal box, cutting cross the folded edge, so that you have a piece of card measuring approximately 10 x 5cm/4 x 2in, with a fold running through the middle. This is your bookmark.

stick on decorative paper Cut out a piece of decorative paper the same size as the bookmark. Place the bookmark flat on the table and use glue to stick the decorative paper to the front. Press the paper flat to make sure the edges are secure, then let the glue dry completely.

cut with scissors Cut all the way around the edges of the bookmark using pinking shears or decorative edging scissors. If you find the card difficult to cut, ask an adult to help you.

finishing Peel the backing paper off the magnets and stick one to each side of the folded bookmark. Press down firmly. The magnets hold the bookmark in place. You could add names to the front of the bookmark if you are giving them to friends or family as gifts.

YOU WILL NEED:
decorative paper (such as
gift wrap) • pencil • ruler •
scissors • PVA/white glue •
1 decorative button •
1 metal brooch back •
strong/tacky glue

cut out paper strips Using
a pencil and ruler, mark four strips
measuring 1.5 x 20cm/¾ x 8in on the
back of your decorative paper. Cut out
the strips with scissors. Lay the strips
on a flat surface with the patterned side
facing downward, overlapping them so
that they form a star shape.

loop and glue strips Fold in the end of one strip
toward the centre so that it forms a loop and stick in place
using glue. Repeat with the other strips so that a looped
flower shape is formed, then allow the glue to dry completely.

attach button When the glue is completely dry,
stick a pretty button to the centre of the flower corsage
and press down firmly to hold it in place.

finishing Turn the flower corsage to
the wrong side and stick on the metal
brooch back using strong/tacky glue.
If you wish to use a hot glue gun, you
will have to ask an adult to help as the
glue gets very hot.

paper corsage

This pretty corsage is made from strips of decorative paper looped together and glued in the centre. Make them from glittery paper and use them to decorate wrapped gifts at Christmas. They also look great made from fabrics such as wool or felt.

printing &
painting

stamped
gift wrap

It's easy to create your own gift wrap, cards and tags using a rubber stamp and inkpad. We chose a old-fashioned biplane motif which we stamped onto plain white photocopier paper to make this smart gift wrap.

YOU WILL NEED:

rubber stamp with motif of
your choice • ink pad • plain
white photocopier paper •
1 piece of white card stock •
scissors • hole punch • narrow
ribbon for gift tag

apply ink to stamp Hold the
stamp in one hand and dab ink onto
the stamp. Apply enough ink to just
cover the motif.

start stamping Place the stamp in position on the paper
and hold firmly in place but rock the sides gently so that the
ink is transferred evenly over the paper. Continue to stamp
at regular intervals until the paper is covered with the motif.

make gift labels Cut out gift tags from white card by cutting a small
rectangle measuring approximately 7 x 4cm/3 x 1½in. Cut the two corners off
the top edge at a 45° angle, then use a hole punch to make a hole in the top.
Use the stamp to print a plane motif in the middle of each tag.

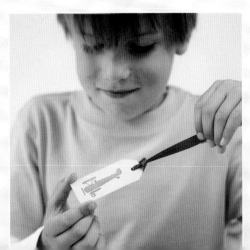

finishing When the ink is dry,
thread the ribbon through the hole
in the gift tag to finish.

YOU WILL NEED:

medium-sized potato • heart-shaped cookie cutter • chopping board • sharp knife • paint • saucers to hold the paint • paper towel • white card stock • paper flowers • strong/tacky glue

cut out shape using cutter

Ask an adult to cut the potato in half, making sure that the surface of the potato is as flat as possible. Place the cookie cutter on a chopping board with the cutting edge facing upwards. Press the potato down on the cutter. Ask an adult to cut away the excess potato using a sharp knife. Remove the cutter.

apply paint If the potato is wet, blot it on a piece of paper towel. Pour some paint onto a saucer and dip the potato in the paint. Make sure the whole shape is covered, but take care not to sink the shape too deep into the paint.

stamp on card Press the potato shape firmly onto the card. To ensure the whole design prints clearly, use a gentle rocking motion, moving the potato from side to side without lifting it from the paper. This will help to apply the paint evenly. Print a second heart shape on the card and leave the paint to dry.

finishing touches When the paint has dried, glue a paper rose to the top of each heart to finish. Let the glue dry completely before writing in the card.

valentine card

Potato-printing is a firm crafting favourite and can be used to decorate everything from wrapping paper and cards to fabric (using fabric paint). We chose a heart-shaped motif and cut it using a cookie cutter to create these pretty Valentine cards.

paper plate animals

Paper plates are a versatile addition to any craft cupboard. In particular, they make great masks. This cute lion mask, complete with a furry pompom nose, is just one example. See overleaf for more fun things to make from paper plates.

YOU WILL NEED:

1 paper plate • brown and yellow paint • paintbrushes • saucer for paint • pencil • scissors • strong/tacky glue • small brown pompom for nose • 1 wooden stick 30cm/12in long

paint plate Apply the yellow paint to the whole plate using a large paintbrush. You may need to apply a second coat of paint for complete coverage. Allow to dry completely.

cut out mane Use the pencil to draw the triangular shapes for the mane around the edge of the plate. Cut out the triangular shapes carefully using scissors. Draw out the two eyes and cut out using scissors. You may want to ask an adult to cut out the eyes using a craft knife.

apply paint Use the brown paint to paint the mane, as well as a border of approximately 2.5cm/1in around the edge of the plate. Apply a further coat of paint if required.

finishing off Use a fine paintbrush to paint the lion's muzzle. Once the paint has dried, stick on the lion's 'nose'. Apply a blob of glue to the pompom and stick it in position above the muzzle. Use strong glue to attach the wooden stick to the back of the mask.

owl

Decorated with fluffy feathers, this cute owl is made from one large and one small paper plate painted dark brown and with a small section cut out to create 'ears'. Finish with a triangular-shaped felt beak and a pair of googly eyes.

elephant

This wise-looking elephant is made from one large paper plate and one smaller plate cut in two for the ears. Both were painted grey and left to dry before the ears were glued in place. Finish with two white tusks snipped from thin card stock. The long trunk was cut from another large paper plate and the eyes and trunk details were simply painted on.

frogs

These wide-mouthed frogs are made by simply folding a green-painted plate in two. Add 3-D-effect googly eyes. We also added a long, red satin ribbon tongue and furry pipe-cleaner legs.

little tips

To prevent the paper plates from wrinkling, use two plates when painting, then remove the second plate from underneath when the paint has dried. Try to avoid using too much paint – two thinner coats of paint will help prevent the paper plates from buckling and wrinkling.

YOU WILL NEED:

1 piece paper 50 x 40cm/20 x 16in (we used textured paper but you can use watercolour paper or plain white paper) • tea bag and water • small sponge • paintbrush • coloured paints • fine black pen

tear paper edges Lay the paper flat on a table and tear the edges of the paper to make them slightly ragged and uneven. Repeat on all four edges of the piece of paper.

apply tea stain Leave a tea bag in bowl of water until it stains the water dark brown. Dip the sponge in the water and squeeze to remove excess water. Dab the sponge all over the paper to stain it. Leave the paper to dry. If the paper dries a paler shade than required, repeat the process.

paint edges of paper Use dark brown paint to carefully paint around the edges of the paper, then leave to dry. This gives the paper a more antique effect. When the edges are dry, you can begin drawing out the island and colouring in your design.

finishing touches Draw out the island in fine black pen, then use coloured pencils or paint to add palm trees, fish and, of course, the position of the treasure. Don't forget to add the clues. Happy treasure hunting!

treasure map

Create this antique-effect treasure map by ageing paper
using tea, water and paint. Draw an island and some
clues to guarantee hours of fun
spent searching for treasure
with friends.

marbled paper

Marbling paper is a very decorative and easy craft, particularly if you use ready-mixed marbling inks, which are available in a good range of colours. Each piece of marbled paper is unique. Use it to cover boxes and notebooks, as well as stationery.

YOU WILL NEED:

marbling inks in different colours • large shallow dish wide enough to hold the paper • stirring stick • A4/letter-sized white paper

add ink Pour about 2.5cm/1in of water into the bowl. Add drops of two or three differently coloured marbling inks to the water. Make sure you only add small amounts of the ink at a time.

stir ink Use a stick to stir the surface of the water. Do not overmix, or the differently coloured inks will blend into one colour. Instead, gently stir the water to create the delicate swirly patterns typical of marbling.

immerse paper Take the sheet of paper and carefully lower it into the bowl so that the whole piece is submerged. Press down lightly with your fingers but be careful not to move the paper around in the bowl.

remove paper Carefully lift the paper out of the bowl and allow excess water and ink to run back into the bowl. Place the paper on a flat surface and leave it to dry completely. Use the marbled paper to cover notebooks and finish with a decorative paper initial.

YOU WILL NEED:

circular lidded box • selection of paper doilies • masking tape • paint • saucer to hold paint • fat paintbrush or stencil brush • paper towel • scissors • PVA/white glue • two lengths of narrow ribbon to fit around the lid • 2 decorative butterflies

stencil lid Place the doily on the box lid in the position to be stencilled. You can use tiny pieces of masking tape to hold the doily securely in place for stencilling. It is important that the doily is not moved during the stencilling process as this will smudge the design. Dip the brush in the paint and remove as much excess paint as possible by wiping the brush on a paper towel.

peel off stencil Once you have covered the whole stencil with paint, allow the paint to dry slightly for a few minutes then carefully peel off the masking tape, if used, and lift the doily stencil off the box lid to reveal the design.

cut out motifs Take a doily and cut out shapes from it using scissors. Different doilies have different designs, so look at them carefully to discover the prettiest shapes to cut out.

finishing Apply glue to the back of the cut-out doily shape and then press it firmly onto the side of the box. Continue sticking the shapes around the box at regular intervals. Stick two lengths of ribbon around the edge of the box lid and press firmly in place and allow to dry. Stick the two decorative butterflies to the lid of the box to finish.

doily box

The delicate lace-like effect of doilies makes them a perfect craft paper and they can be cut up and used to decorate many different objects, including boxes, books and picture frames. Doilies also make great stencils with their delicate lacy shapes, and this plain box combines both stencilling and cut-out doily motifs.

doily cards

These pretty cards are stencilled using the edges of doilies to show their lace-effect borders and finished with cute felt flowers.

doily box

This tiny cardboard box is trimmed with a border of self-adhesive paper lace and a flower made by pleating a doily to form a three-dimensional shape.

doily picture frames

Shapes cut from a selection of doilies are used to decorate these pretty wooden picture frames painted in shades of pink and lilac. Paint the frames your chosen colour and allow to dry. Stick on the cutout doily shapes using PVA/white glue.

little tips

Cheaper paper doilies are less intricate, so it is worth spending a bit more to get some really pretty ones to use. You can also find pretty self-adhesive paper lace trims at good craft shops.

YOU WILL NEED:

assorted textured papers and card (we used corrugated card) • plain paper • coloured pencils • woven table mat • paper for template • scissors • pencil • plain coloured card stock for background • PVA/white glue • picture frame • paint (optional)

start rubbing Choose a piece of textured card or paper. Place a sheet of white paper over the card and rub a coloured pencil quickly over the surface of the paper, so the texture is picked up in coloured pencil.

continue rubbing Place the paper over the woven table mat and rub the coloured pencil over the surface of the paper. Now rub the pencil in the opposite direction so that you can see the textured weave of the mat. You may wish to use two different coloured pencils for this.

cut out shapes Photocopy the flower, leaf and pot shapes on page 120 onto a piece of plain paper and cut them out. Place the templates onto the back of the rubbed papers and draw around them in pencil. Each flower needs approximately six petals. Now cut the shapes out.

finishing Stick the leaf, flower and pot shapes to a plain piece of card stock and allow the glue to dry completely. You may wish to add glitter, beads or buttons for extra decoration. If desired, paint the picture frame to match the flowers. Fit the picture inside the frame to finish.

rubbings collage

Younger children in particular will enjoy the craft of rubbing – you can do this using a variety of objects. We used different textured papers and card, but coins, wallpaper, bark and buttons also work well.

modelling

papier-mâché pig

This jolly pink pig is made using the classic papier-mâché technique. Painted a fetching shade of pink and finished with a curly pipe-cleaner tail, he would make a great gift for a friend or sibling. You could even paint a name on the side to personalize the gift.

YOU WILL NEED:

balloon • newspaper • bowl • PVA/white glue • water • brush for glue • egg carton • masking tape (2.5cm/1in wide) • pink and black paint • paintbrushes • felt for ears • pipe cleaner • pencil • strong/tacky glue

stick paper strips Tear the newspaper into 2.5 x 6cm/1 x 3in strips. Squeeze some glue into a bowl and add an equal amount of water to thin the glue. Brush a thin layer of the mixture onto an area of the balloon about 10cm/4in square. Start sticking strips of paper to the balloon. Continue applying glue and paper to the balloon until the surface is entirely covered.

attach legs and snout Apply about three layers of papier mâché and leave to partially dry. Cut out five cups from the egg carton for the pig's legs and snout. Using masking tape, fix the four legs to the underside of the balloon and the snout to the front, covering the balloon knot. Continue covering the balloon with another two or three layers of papier mâché, so the balloon, legs and snout are completely covered. Leave to dry completely – this will take at least a day and possibly more.

decorate pig Paint the pig pale pink. You may need to apply two or three coats of paint to achieve good coverage. Use black paint and a fine brush to depict the trotters, eyes and nose and leave to dry completely. Cut two ear shapes from felt or paper and glue them to the balloon just above the pig's eyes.

finishing Wrap a light brown pipe cleaner around a pencil to form a coil shape. Gently pull on the coil to open it out a little. Pierce a hole in the back of the pig using scissors (you may want to ask an adult to do this). Push one end of the tail into the hole and apply a blob of strong/tacky glue to fix it in position.

octopus

Cut the bottom off a balloon covered in dried papier mâché to create this leggy octopus. Painted green and finished with googly eyes and pipe-cleaner legs, he makes a fun addition to any shelf or window ledge!

hot air balloon

Use a standard balloon to make this bold hot air balloon. The balloon was painted in quarter sections in bright red and turquoise. The basket is made from a paper cup attached to the balloon with narrow ribbon. Hang the balloon from your bedroom light for a cool addition to your bedroom.

sausage dog

Use a long sausage-shaped balloon with egg-carton legs to make this cute dog. He has long felt ears, a pompom nose, a ribbon collar and a pipe cleaner tail.

little tips

Remember that the more layers of papier mâché that you apply, the more robust your finished item will be. Make sure all the layers are completely dry before painting.

YOU WILL NEED:

strips of thick decorated paper (measuring 20 x 2cm/8 x 1in for largest star) • headband • strong/tacky glue

form knot shape Make a knot approximately a third of the way along one strip of paper. Pull as firmly as you can without the paper tearing and press the knot flat between your fingers to form a five-sided pentagon, with the two long paper ends sticking out from two of the five sides.

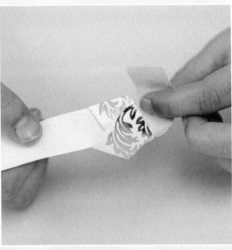

fold paper Fold the shorter end of the paper across the pentagon shape and press flat with your finger. Tuck the end of the paper inside the fold created by the knot on the inside of the pentagon shape.

continue folding Fold the remaining longer length of paper over the pentagon shape, following the shape of the pentagon. Fold the end of the paper inside the pentagon shape to finish.

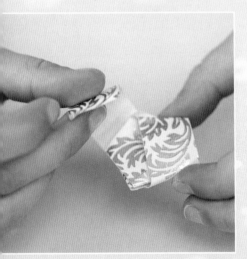

finishing Use your thumbnail to gently push in the flat folded edges of the pentagon shape and to gently coax the shape into becoming a more 3–D star shape. Try blowing gently inside the star to further inflate the shape and to puff it up more. Make a selection of different-sized stars and use glue to stick them to the headband.

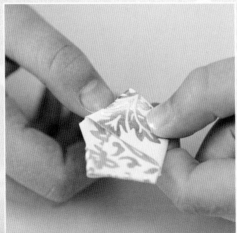

star headband

This pretty headband is decorated with delicate paper stars made by folding lengths of narrow paper. We used a selection of different-sized stars which were then stuck onto a headband.

egg-carton insects

Another versatile and inexpensive craft essential, the egg carton can be used to make many items, such as these long-legged ants with their huge eyes and pipe-cleaner legs. You could make a whole army of them and share them with friends!

YOU WILL NEED:

egg carton • scissors • brown paint • paintbrush • 4 brown pipe cleaners • strong/tacky glue • 2 small papier-mâché beads • googly eyes

paint egg carton Use scissors to cut out two sections of the egg carton. Paint the carton using brown paint and leave it to dry completely. You may need to apply a second coat of paint for complete coverage.

glue on legs Cut six equal lengths of brown pipe cleaner, each measuring approximately 10cm/4in. Glue three lengths of pipe cleaner along one side of the egg-box carton at equal spaces, then repeat on the other side. Bend the legs to adjust them so that the ant can stand up easily.

stick on eyes Paint the papier-mâché beads the same brown as the ant's body and leave to dry. Glue them to the front of the ant. Now glue a pair of googly eyes on top of the papier-mâché beads and allow to dry.

finishing Use an awl or a cocktail stick to pierce two holes just above the eyes. Insert two lengths of pipe cleaner approximately 3cm/1⅛in long. These are the antennae. If necessary, apply a blob of glue to the inside of the head to hold them in place.

YOU WILL NEED:

(for the chest of drawers)

4 small empty matchboxes • glue • 2 different shades of paint • paintbrush • strong/tacky glue • 4 small beads for feet • 4 small clear beads for knobs

stick matchboxes together

Apply a layer of glue to the bottom of the first matchbox and stick to one of the other matchboxes, pressing down firmly. Continue sticking until the four matchboxes are joined together. Allow the glue to dry completely.

paint matchboxes Paint the outside of the matchboxes and allow to dry completely. You may need to apply a second coat of paint for complete coverage.

paint drawers Paint the four drawers using the second shade of paint and leave to dry completely. Again, you may need to apply a second coat of paint for complete coverage.

finishing Dab a blob of glue on the base of each metallic bead and stick to the base of the matchboxes, pressing down firmly with your finger until all four are in place. Now glue a clear bead to the front of each drawer. You may find it easier to ask an adult to stick the beads on for you using a hot glue gun.

dolls' house furniture

This delightful collection of dolls' house
furniture is made from recycled matchboxes,
cardboard and craft sticks painted in bright
colours and decorated with patterned
origami papers and beads.

dressing table

Made using eight small matchboxes with a thick cardboard top, this dressing table also features a decorative matching mirror made using a piece of painted card and a mirror cut from kitchen foil.

wardrobe

This freestanding wardrobe was made from a large box of matches. The front of the box was cut in half to create doors. The wardrobe was painted to match the dressing table and has metal feet and bead knobs to finish.

dolls' house bed

A large matchbox was also used to make this dolls' house bed. The headboard is made from large and medium craft sticks painted to match the other furniture. A sheet of prettily patterned origami paper makes a decorative bedcover and pillow.

little tips

Ask your parents to collect different-sized and shaped matchboxes from hotels and bars to keep in your craft box or cupboard. They come in many different shapes and sizes, and the cardboard is often of better quality than standard matchboxes.

YOU WILL NEED:

bowl to use as mould • clingfilm/plastic wrap • sticky/adhesive tape • 8 sheets tissue paper • paintbrush • PVA/white glue • decorative butterfly

cover bowl Place the bowl upside down on a flat surface and cover with a layer of clingfilm/plastic wrap. Pull the clingfilm/plastic wrap tight, then fold the edges to the inside of the bowl and press to the sides. Use sticky tape to hold it in place, if necessary.

tear tissue paper Tear the tissue paper into small strips measuring approximately 2 x 4cm/1 x 2in in length. You may wish to put all the tissue-paper strips in a bowl while you are working on the papier mâché.

start sticking Place a piece of tissue paper on the bowl and use a paintbrush to spread a fine layer of PVA/white glue over it. Continue to place strips of tissue paper all over the bowl and paint with glue. Build up layers of tissue paper until the bowl is completely covered. You will need at least ten layers of tissue paper and more will be required to create a thicker bowl.

finishing Allow the papier mâché to dry completely before attempting to remove it. This will take at least a day and possibly more, depending upon conditions. When the papier mâché is completely dry, ease it off the bowl and stick on a sparkling butterfly to finish.

tissue-paper bowl

This delicate bowl is made using the traditional papier-mâché technique, but with layers of tissue paper and PVA/white glue instead of the usual newspaper and paste. The jewel tones of the tissue paper are perfect for this method, creating a dainty bowl that makes a good gift.

fun flowers

Layers of coloured card, ric rac trim and buttons are combined to make these vibrant flowers with stems fashioned from drinking straws. Make a group of them to create a striking bouquet in a vase as a Mother's Day gift.

YOU WILL NEED:

plain paper • scissors • pencil •
pieces of coloured card stock •
glue • coloured paper • ric rac
trim • decorative buttons •
coloured drinking straws •
sticky tape

create template Photocopy the
templates on page 120–121 and cut
them out. Place a template on the back
of a piece of coloured card stock and
draw around it in pencil. You need two
different colours of card per flower.

cut out flowers Cut out the flowers carefully using
scissors. You may find it easier to cut out all the flowers
at once and decorate them together. Use scallop-edged
scissors or pinking shears for a more decorative effect.

start decorating Stick one flower shape on top of another, making sure
that the petals from the lower flower sit between those of the top flower. Now
snip circles from coloured paper and stick them onto each flower and petal.

finishing Cut short lengths of ric rac
trim and glue to the flower between
the centre and each petal. Glue a button
to the centre of the flower and one to
each petal. Stick the drinking straw
stem to the back of the flower using
sticky tape, or ask an adult to do this
using a hot glue gun.

YOU WILL NEED:
6 sheets of tissue paper
per flower • pipe cleaner •
scissors • ribbon for hanging

start folding Place the sheets of tissue paper flat on the table in front of you. Starting at the end closest to you, fold the paper concertina-style into folds that are 2cm/¾in wide. Press each fold flat. You could leave the pleated paper under a heavy book overnight to make it as flat as possible, or ask an adult to run a hot iron over the pleats.

tie paper in middle Mark the centre of the folded paper by folding it in half. Next tie the pipe cleaner around the this point and pull it as tightly as you can, gathering the paper together. Twist the ends of the pipe cleaner together and trim the loose ends using scissors. Now tie one end of a length of ribbon around the centre of the folded paper so you can hang up the finished flower.

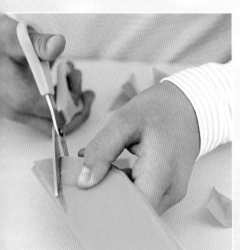

cut ends Make a curved petal shape at the end of each flower by cutting a gentle curve approximately 4cm/1½in in from one end of the tissue paper. Repeat at the other end of the tissue paper.

finishing Gently unfold the pleats of the tissue paper and coax them out into a flower shape. This takes some time and needs to be done very gently and carefully to avoid tearing the delicate paper. Hang the flowers in clusters above a party table.

tissue-paper blooms

These giant paper flowers are made from layers of folded tissue paper and are a cheap and easy yet striking decoration for any party or special occasion. Make them in several sizes and hang them from the ceiling using lengths of ribbon.

space rocket

This colourful rocket is made from the cardboard tube inside a roll of paper towels. Decorate with bright paper and tissue-paper flames ready for take off!

YOU WILL NEED:

1 cardboard tube • plain paper •
PVA/white glue • decorative
paper • thin card stock •
cardboard pot or peat pot for
base • tissue paper for flames •
glue • paint

cover tube Cut a piece of paper
to fit the cardboard tube and add
on 2.5cm/1in to the longer edge for
overlapping. Fold the paper around
the tube and glue in place along the
edge. Allow the glue to dry.

glue on shapes Cut a selection of rectangular shapes
approximately 2 x 3cm/1 x 1½in from the decorative paper.
Apply glue to the back of each shape and stick them to the
card roll, pressing each piece flat as you go.

make nose cone From the card stock, cut out a semicircle with
a 15cm/6in diameter. Fold the piece of card into a cone shape and
glue in place along the edge. Glue the cone to the top of the tube.

finishing Cut out triangles from the
top edge of a peat pot to create a fin
shape, then paint the fins and allow
them to dry. Glue the fins to the base of
the cone. Cut out lengths of orange and
red tissue paper measuring 30 x 1.5cm/
12 x 1in and glue them to the inside of
the base to create the rocket's flames.

YOU WILL NEED:

Instant papier-mâché mix
(Celluclay or similar) • water •
mixing bowl • cocktail sticks •
paint in a variety of colours •
paintbrushes • elastic nylon
thread • scissors

form beads Make up the papier-mâché mix as directed on the packet. The resulting paste should be fairly dry, so it can be easily formed into balls. Take a lump of the paste and roll it together between the palms of your hands to form the beads.

pierce beads Push a cocktail stick through the centre of each bead. This will create a hole for thread and will keep it open as the paper pulp dries out. Once you have finished making and piercing all the beads, leave them to dry, which can take as long as a couple of days.

decorate beads Paint the beads in different shades and leave them to dry. The cocktail sticks come in handy for holding the beads while painting them. Allow the paint to dry and then use a fine paintbrush to decorate the beads with tiny spots in contrasting colours.

thread beads Gently remove the cocktail sticks from the beads then thread the beads onto elastic nylon thread. When you have reached the desired length, knot the ends of the thread and trim the ends using scissors.

beaded
necklace

This adorable necklace is made of beads formed from paper pulp, which is available from most craft shops. Painted in bright colours and decorated with contrasting spots they make delightful gifts for little girls.

toy town

Recycle empty juice cartons, cereal boxes and cardboard tubes by painting them in cheery shades to create buildings for this cute toy town. Use scraps of paper in bold hues to make windows and doors and screwed-up tissue paper for trees.

YOU WILL NEED:

large carton or box (to create basic house) • white paint • paintbrush • scissors • scraps of paper for windows and doors • PVA/white glue • card for roof • sticky/adhesive tape

paint box Using a thick paintbrush, paint the box in your chosen shade. Let the paint dry completely. For the best results, apply a second coat of paint and let it dry.

add door and windows Once the box is dry, cut out squares of paper in contrasting colours to create a door and windows. Glue them in place.

add detail Use a fine paintbrush and contrasting-coloured paint to add the window frames and door decorations. Allow the paint to dry completely.

finishing Cut a piece of card measuring 22cm/9in long by the width of the box. Fold the card 3 times to form a triangle shape and use tape to hold the edges together. Use a paintbrush to paint on the roof tiles. Allow the paint to dry completely before glueing the flat base of the roof to the top of the box to finish.

YOU WILL NEED:

paper for template • pencil •
stiff cardboard • scissors •
eraser • paint • paintbrush •
black marker pen

make template Photocopy the
dinosaur templates on pages 120–121
and cut them out. Place the templates
on the back of the cardboard and draw
around them in pencil, making sure you
mark the slits exactly as they appear on
the original templates. You will need one
main body section, two body sections
and two side sections.

cut out dinosaur Cut out the five dinosaur sections
and carefully cut along the slit lines as marked on the
templates. These are the slits that enable the different
parts to be slotted together. Use a rubber to remove the
pencil marks on the back of the card before painting.

paint dinosaur Lay out all the sections flat on a table and begin painting
markings in the first colour and leave to dry. Continue painting markings in the
remaining colours and leave to dry. Once the paint is dry, repeat on the other
side of the card and leave that side to dry completely.

finishing Assemble the dinosaur
by slotting the sections together. Start
with the main body section, slide up
the two body sections, then slot on the
two side sections. Once the dinosaur is
constructed, finish by drawing on eyes
and a mouth using a black marker pen.

3-D dinosaur

Make this friendly 3-D dinosaur using layers of cardboard decorated in shades of green and brown and simply slotted together.

templates

The outlines shown on pages 118-123 have been reduced in size so they fit on these pages. Before cutting out the templates, enlarge them on a photocopier by 200 per cent to make them the right size.

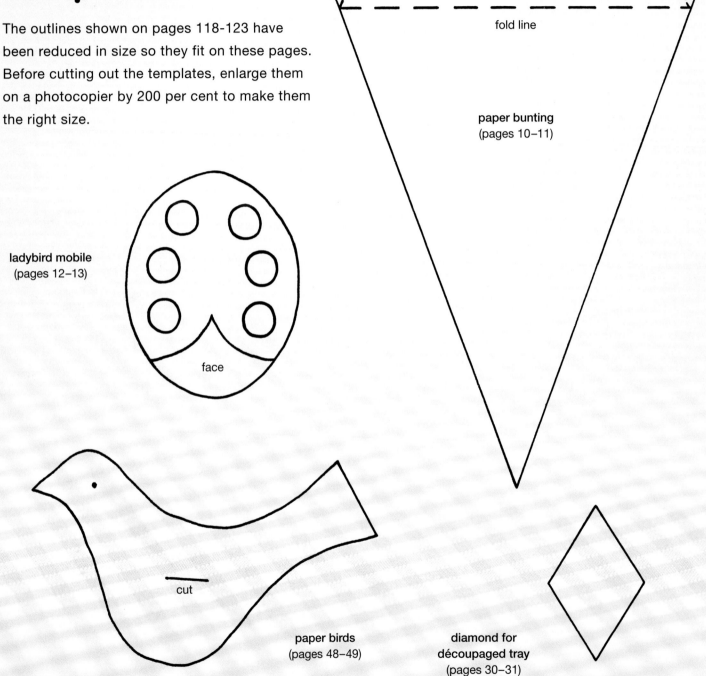

fold line

paper bunting
(pages 10–11)

ladybird mobile
(pages 12–13)

face

cut

paper birds
(pages 48–49)

diamond for
découpaged tray
(pages 30–31)

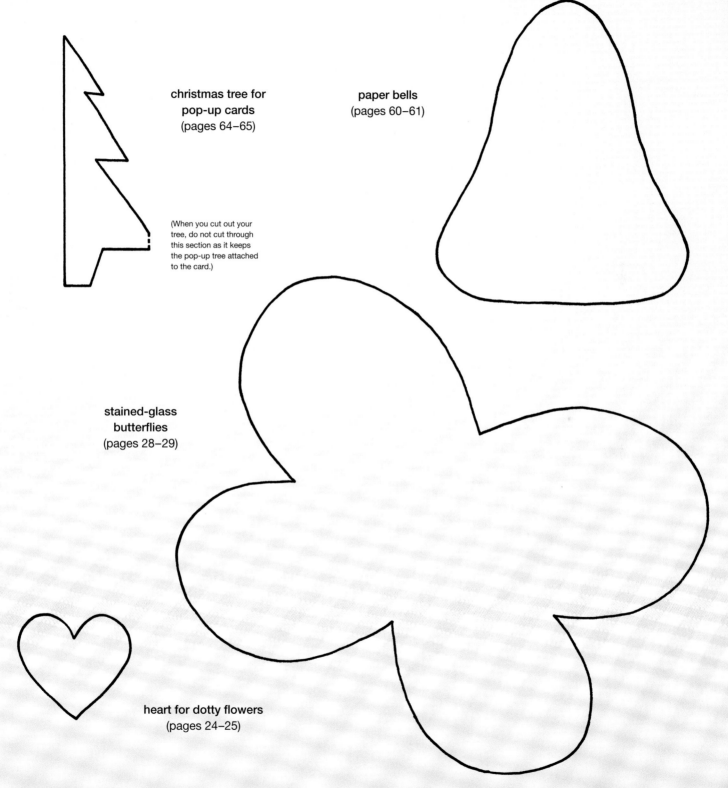

**christmas tree for
pop-up cards**
(pages 64–65)

(When you cut out your
tree, do not cut through
this section as it keeps
the pop-up tree attached
to the card.)

paper bells
(pages 60–61)

**stained-glass
butterflies**
(pages 28–29)

heart for dotty flowers
(pages 24–25)

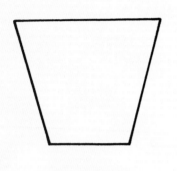

flower pot for
rubbings collage
(pages 88–89)

petal and leaf for
rubbings collage
(pages 88–89)

large flat flowers
(pages 106–107)

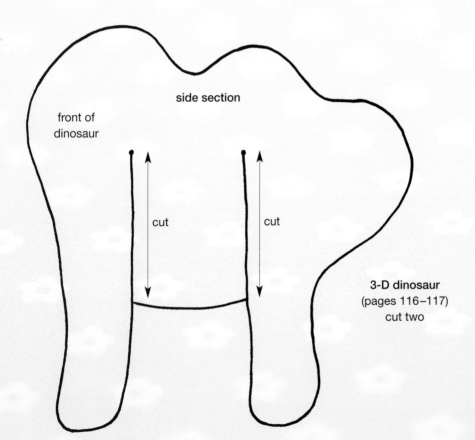

side section

front of
dinosaur

cut

cut

3-D dinosaur
(pages 116–117)
cut two

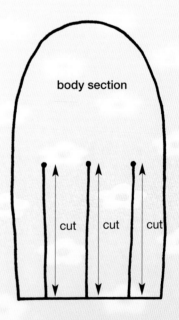

body section

cut   cut   cut

3-D dinosaur
(pages 116–117)
cut two

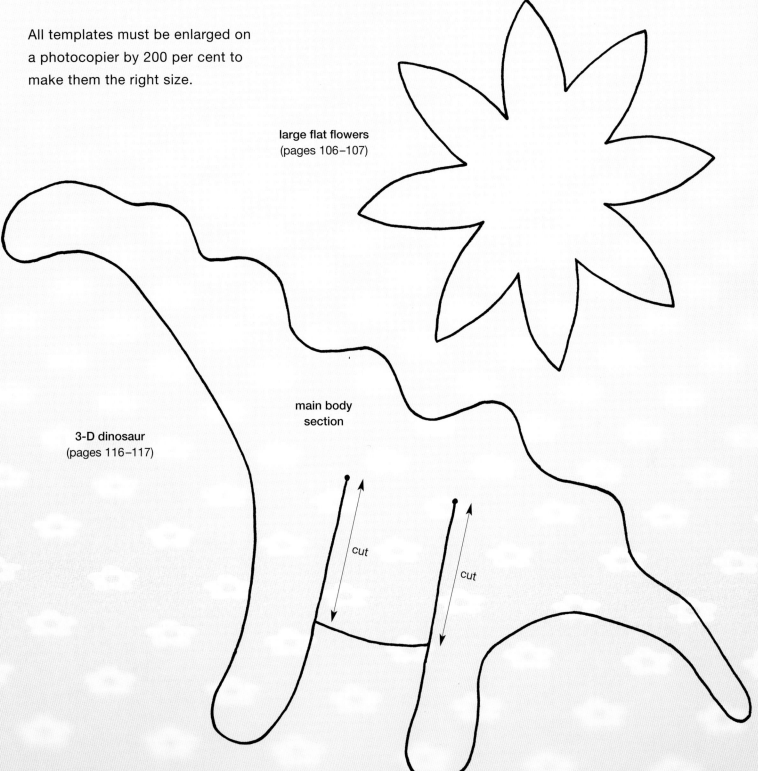

All templates must be enlarged on a photocopier by 200 per cent to make them the right size.

large flat flowers
(pages 106–107)

3-D dinosaur
(pages 116–117)

main body
section

cut

cut

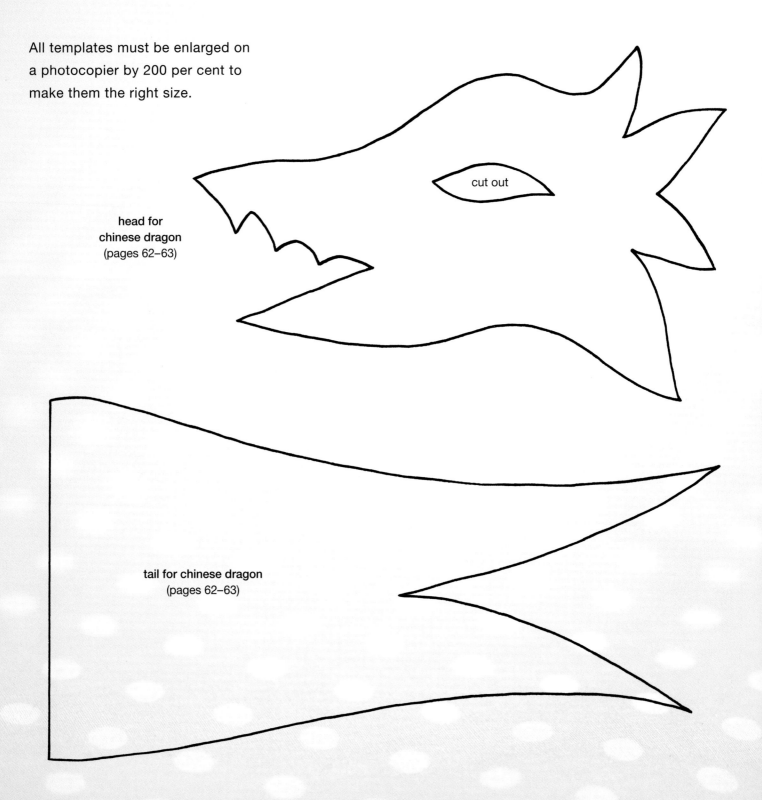

All templates must be enlarged on a photocopier by 200 per cent to make them the right size.

head for
chinese dragon
(pages 62–63)

cut out

tail for chinese dragon
(pages 62–63)

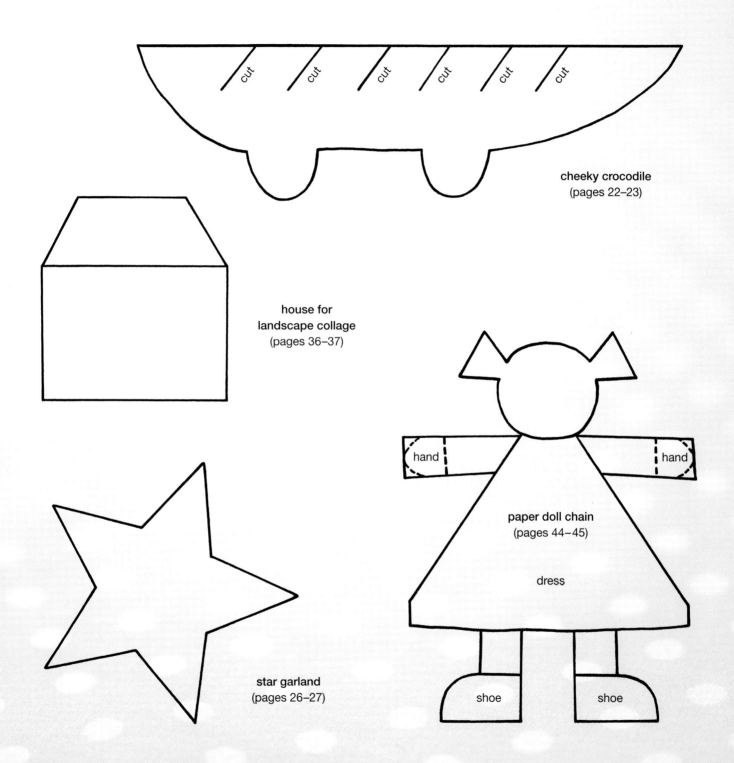

cut cut cut cut cut cut

cheeky crocodile
(pages 22–23)

house for
landscape collage
(pages 36–37)

hand hand

paper doll chain
(pages 44–45)

dress

star garland
(pages 26–27)

shoe shoe

UK sources

BAKER ROSS

www.bakerross.co.uk

Marbling inks.

B&Q

Visit www.diy.com for your nearest store.

Wooden battens and lining paper.

CALICO CRAFTS

www.calicocrafts.co.uk

Decorative paper, craft punches and embellishments.

CREATIONS ART AND CRAFT MATERIALS

www.ecreations.co.uk

Stencils, paints, brushes, and glues as well as plain and decorative papers and card and a large selection of rubber stamps.

EARLY LEARNING CENTRE

Visit www.elc.co.uk for your nearest store.

Good selection of crafting supplies for younger children.

THE ENGLISH STAMP COMPANY

www.englishstamp.com
01929 439117

Great selection of rubber stamps, which can be customized to include your child's name or address. Also coloured stamping inks.

GREAT LITTLE TRADING COMPANY

www.gltc.co.uk

Ready-mixed paint, art folders and "paint your own" kits.

HOBBYCRAFT

Visit www.hobbycraft.co.uk for your nearest store.

Chain of craft superstores carrying everything the younger crafter needs.

HOMECRAFTS DIRECT

www.homecrafts.co.uk
Good selection of plain paper and card as well as tissue paper in bright jewel shades and instant papier-mâché mix.

IKEA

Visit www.ikea.com for your nearest store.

Wooden boxes, tins and frames for decorating.

JOHN LEWIS

Visit www.johnlewis.com for your nearest store.

Buttons, ric rac and ribbon.

LAKELAND

www.lakeland.co.uk

Doilies in different shapes and sizes.

LONDON GRAPHIC CENTRE

Visit www.londongraphics.co.uk for your nearest store.

Card, board and paper, pens and markers, paints and brushes, glue and pencils.

MUJI

Visit www.muji.co.uk for your nearest store.

Plain boxes and notebooks, which are ideal for covering or for découpage.

PAPERCHASE

Visit www.paperchase.co.uk for your nearest store.

Handmade papers, gift wrap, tissue paper and card plus plain cards and envelopes in a rainbow of colours.

SEWING AND CRAFT SUPERSTORE

296–312 Balham High Road
London SW17 7AA
020 8767 0036
www.craftysewer.com

Everything from beads and sequins to blank cards, felt, pompoms, wool, buttons and pipe cleaners.

THE STENCIL LIBRARY

Stocksfield Hall
Northumberland
NE43 7TN
01661 844844
www.stencil-library.com

Great selection of stencils from simple designs to large complex motifs.

US sources

BRITEX FABRICS
146 Geary Street
San Francisco, CA 94108
415 392 2910
www.britexfabrics.com

Ribbons, trims, and notions.

**THE BUTTON EMPORIUM
& RIBBONRY**
1016 S.W. Taylor Street
Portland, OR 97205

503 228 6372
www.buttonemporium.com

*Vintage and assorted
decorative buttons.*

DICK BLICK
Visit www.dickblick.com for
your nearest store.

*Cardmaking supplies, crepe,
tissue, and decorative paper,
stencils, ribbon, and more.*

**HEART OF THE HOME
STENCILS**
www.stencils4u.com

*Alphabet stencils as well as
other simple designs for kids.*

HOBBY LOBBY
Visit www.hobbylobby.com
for your nearest store.

Arts and crafts stores.

IKEA
Visit www.ikea.com for your
nearest store.

*Unpainted wooden photo
frames, plain tins for
découpaging, and cute
accessories.*

JAM PAPER
Visit www.jampaper.com for
your nearest store

*Every kind of paper and
card stock.*

JOANN FABRICS
Visit www.joann.com for your
nearest store.

*A wide selection of
scrapbooking materials.*

KARI ME AWAY
www.karimeaway.com

*Cute novelty buttons, ric rac
trim, and glass beads.*

KATE'S PAPERIE
72 Spring Street
New York, NY 10012
212 941 9816
Visit www.katespaperie.com
for their other stores.

Cute rubber stamps for kids.

MICHAELS
Visit www.michaels.com for
your nearest store.

*Every kind of art and craft
material, including beads,
stamps, hole punches, ink
pads, embellishments, glue,
and natural wood frames.*

PAPER CREATIONS
www.papercreations.com

*Supplies for papercrafting
and scrapbooking as well
as rubber stamps.*

PAPER SOURCE
www.paper-source.com

*Great selection of decorative
papers, as well as crafting
basics such as scissors,
glue, and hole punches.*

PAPER WISHES
www.paperwishes.com

*Paper, scrapbooks, stamping
accessories, stickers, tools,
and more.*

**PEARL ART AND CRAFTS
SUPPLIES**
Visit www.pearlpaint.com for
your nearest store.

*Brushes, modelling clay,
adhesives, papers, and card.*

PRIZM
The Artist's Supply Store
5690 Mayfield Rd.
Lyndhurst, OH 44124
440 605 9434
www.prizmart.com

Paints, paper, and more.

TARGET
Visit www.target.com for your
nearest store.

*Paper, scrapbooking
accessories, tools, and more.*

UTRECHT
Visit www.utrechtart.com for
your nearest store.

*Quality artists' materials
and supplies. Natural wood
frames, paints, craft paper
and blank notecards.*

picture credits

ALL PHOTOGRAPHY BY POLLY WREFORD

page 10–11 decorative scrapbooking paper and scissors from The Sewing and Craft Superstore; satin ribbon from Hobbycraft; **page 12–13** coloured card, glue and brushes from The Sewing and Craft Superstore; balsa wood and nylon thread from Hobbycraft; **page 14–15** Black card, striped scrapbooking paper, black paint and buttons from The Sewing and Craft Superstore; picture frame from IKEA; **page 16–17** blank box, gingham ribbon and ric rac trim from Hobbycraft; notebook from Paperchase; felt braid and velvet ribbon from The Sewing and Craft Superstore; **page 18–19** paper and self-adhesive dots from Paperchase; ric rac trim, glue and decorative buttons from The Sewing and Craft Superstore; **page 20–21** blank box from Hobbycraft; notebook and paper from Paperchase; felt braid and ric rac trim from The Sewing and Craft Superstore; **page 22–23** card, googly eyes, paint and paintbrushes from The Sewing and Craft Superstore; **page 24–25** card and braid flowers from The Sewing and Craft Superstore; self-adhesive dots from Paperchase; paper cups from John Lewis; **page 26–27** card, glue, glitter, ribbon and large needle from The Sewing and Craft Superstore; **page 28–29** black card and glue from The Sewing and Craft Superstore; white pencil and coloured tissue paper (available in quires) from Paperchase; **page 30–31** origami papers from Paperchase, similar tray from IKEA; **page 32–33** decorative papers, ric rac and buttons from The Sewing and Craft Superstore; frame from IKEA; **page 34–35** hole punch, card and felt braid from The Sewing and Craft Superstore; **page 36–37** paper and card, paints and brushes from The Sewing and Craft Superstore; tissue paper from Paperchase; **page 38–39** paint, buttons, ribbons and ric rac trim from The Sewing and Craft Superstore; **page 40–41** card, decorative paper and pipe cleaners from The Sewing and Craft Superstore; **page 42–43** plain paper and black pen from Paperchase; **page 44–45** plain paper from IKEA; gingham ribbon and marker pens from The Sewing and Craft Superstore; dotted and patterned origami papers from Paperchase; **page 46–47** paper from Paperchase; pens and glitter from The Sewing and Craft Superstore; wood from B&Q; **page 48–49** card, marker pen and origami paper from Paperchase; **page 50–51** paper from Paperchase; **page 52–53** dotted paper from The Sewing and Craft Superstore; **page 54–55** coloured card, ric rac and felt braid from The Sewing and Craft Superstore; **page 56–57** paper from Paperchase; pipe cleaners and googly eyes from The Sewing and

Craft Superstore; **page 58–59** paper and card from Paperchase; skull and crossbones stamp and ink from The English Stamp Company; **page 60–61** scrapbooking papers, beads, ribbon and bells from The Sewing and Craft Superstore; **page 62–62** card and paint from The Sewing and Craft Superstore; tissue paper from Paperchase; narrow wooden battens from B&Q; **page 64–65** blank cards, paint and brushes from Hobbycraft; **page 66–67** wrapping paper from John Lewis; self-adhesive magnets (can be cut to size) from The Sewing and Craft Superstore; **page 68–69** scrapbooking paper, button and brooch back from The Sewing and Craft Superstore; **page 70–71** paper plates from John Lewis; googly eyes, paint and pipe cleaners from The Sewing and Craft Superstore; picture frame from IKEA; **page 72–73** aeroplane rubber stamp and ink from The English Stamp Company; ribbon from Hobbycraft; **page 74–75** plain cards, miniature roses and cookie cutter from Hobbycraft; **page 76–77** paint, brushes and pompoms from The Sewing and Craft Superstore; **page 78–79** paint, feathers, googly eyes and paintbrushes from The Sewing and Craft Superstore; **page 80–81** textured paper and pens from Paperchase; ribbon from Hobbycraft; **page 82–83** marbling inks from Baker Ross; origami paper used for letter from Paperchase; **page 84–85** paint, ribbon and butterflies from The Sewing and Craft Superstore; paper doilies from Lakeland Ltd; **page 86–87** blank cards, small lidded box and felt decorations from The Sewing and Craft Superstore; paper doilies from Lakeland Ltd; picture frames from IKEA; **page 88–89** paper from The Sewing and Craft Superstore; pencils from Paperchase; frame from IKEA; **page 92–93** PVA glue, pipe cleaners, paint and brushes from The Sewing and Craft Superstore; **page 94–95** paint, pipe cleaners and ribbon from; paper cup (for balloon base) from Hobbycraft; **page 96–97** decorative paper from Paperchase; **page 98–99** pipe cleaners, paint and googly eyes from The Sewing and Craft Superstore; **page 100–101** origami papers from Paperchase; paint, beads and large craft sticks from The Sewing and Craft Superstore; **page 102–103** origami papers from Paperchase; paint, beads and large craft sticks from The Sewing and Craft Superstore; **page 104–105** tissue paper from Paperchase; decorative butterflies from Hobbycraft; **page 106–107** card, buttons, ric rac trim from The Sewing and Craft Superstore; **page 108–109** tissue paper and satin ribbon (by the reel) from Paperchase; **page 110–111** dotted wrapping paper from John Lewis; plain paper and tissue paper from Paperchase; **page 112–113** papier mâché mix and paint from The Sewing and Craft Superstore; **page 114–115** card, paint, brushes and corrugated paper from The Sewing & Craft Superstore; **page 116–117** card and paint from The Sewing & Craft Superstore.

index

acknowledgments

Thank you very much to Polly Wreford for her stunning photography and her unfailing enthusiasm for this project. Thanks also to Annabel Morgan, Sonya Nathoo and Toni Kay for their help at all stages of the book – its design, layout and words. Thank you to The English Stamp Company for their great stamps and inks. Big thanks are also due to all the wonderful models we photographed, for their great patience and enjoyment of the projects. Finally, a big thank you to my husband Michael and my daughters Jessica and Anna for all their help and suggestions for this book.

Ryland Peters & Small would like to thank all the children who modelled for this book, including Anita, Arlo, Arthur, Ava, Beatrice, Bella, Cameron, Elliot, Emma, Helny, Hope, Jack, Kiri, Lily and Loui, Maddie, Max, Maya, Millie, Mimmo, Nathan, Polly and Will.